BUFFALO BILL

NANCY ROBISON

A FIRST BOOK
FRANKLIN WATTS
NEW YORK LONDON TORONTO SYDNEY
1991

Cover photographs courtesy of:
Buffalo Bill Historical Center, Cody, Wy. and Historical Pictures Service, Chicago,
Photographs courtesy of: The Bettmann Archive: pp. 2, 6, 13;
The Buffalo Bill Historical Center, Cody, Wy.: pp. 10, 17, 29, 37,
41, 44, 51 top, 52, 56, 57, 60; Historical Picture Service:
pp. 14, 23, 24, 31, 35, 46, 58 bottom; Brown Brothers: pp. 51
bottom, 58 top.

Library of Congress Cataloging-in-Publication Data

Robison, Nancy.
Buffalo Bill / by Nancy Robison.
p.   cm.—(A First book)
Includes bibliographical references and index.
Summary: Examines the life and times of the frontiersman whose
many careers included Pony Express rider, Indian fighter, scout, and
star of his own Wild West Show.
ISBN 0-531-20007-8
1. Buffalo Bill, 1846–1917—Juvenile literature.   2. Pioneers—
West (U.S.)—Biography—Juvenile literature.   3. Entertainers—
United States—Biography—Juvenile literature.   4. Buffalo Bill's
Wild West Show—History—Juvenile literature.   [1. Buffalo Bill,
1846–1917.   2. West (U.S.)—Biography.]   I. Title.   II. Series.
F594.B63R63   1991
978'.02'092—dc20   90-47221 CIP AC
[B]

CONTENTS

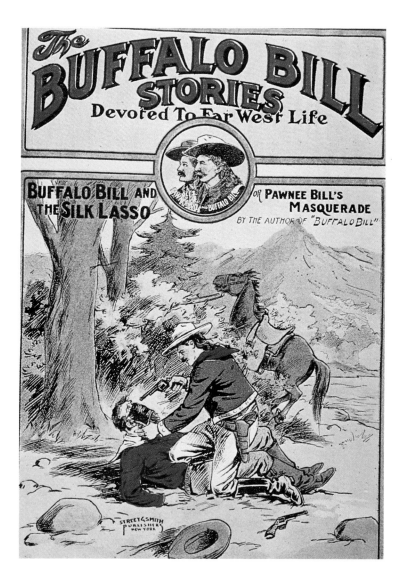

Buffalo Bill captures the outlaw on this cover of a novel. Illustrations like this one strengthened the Buffalo Bill legend.

INTRODUCTION

Buffalo Bill played a dramatic part in shaping the American West. As a young man, he became a scout and guide for the United States military, a Pony Express rider, a hunter, an author, and a showman. And he was a hero to millions of children. Through his traveling Wild West show, he presented a visual panorama of early life in the American West.

Ned Buntline, an author of dime novels, helped make Buffalo Bill famous. Stretching the truth to make a good story, he told of a young man who rode hundreds of miles without a drink of water and walked a thousand miles across the plains. Some of his stories were quite fantastic, but even Bill began to believe they were true, and exaggerated them when telling his own life story.

BUFFALO HUNTER

THE WEST IN 1846 was a rough place in which to live. There were gunfights, Indian battles, natural dangers and hardships, and miles and miles of great isolation. Into all this was born William Frederick Cody, a person who will always be associated with the old West.

Cody earned the nickname "Buffalo Bill" for hunting buffalo for the railroad workers to eat. At the time there were millions of buffalo, and it was common to kill twelve or so a day.

Bill's hunting horse was named "Brigham," after Brigham Young, a Mormon leader. He bought

Buffalo Bill only hunted buffalo for food, not for sport as some people would do later.

it from a Ute Indian. It was a fast horse but not a handsome one. Everyone made fun of Bill's ugly horse. One day, while Bill was hunting, he met five army officers from Fort Hays. They were after buffalo tongues. The officers said they would give him the meat after they killed the buffalo. Bill pretended not to know anything about hunting and just let the officers talk. Actually, he knew plenty.

In the distance eleven buffalo were heading for the creek. The officers made a dash for the animals. Bill started for the creek to head them off. The officers laughed at him and his ugly horse. Then Bill took the blinders off Brigham, and the horse tore out at top speed, running alongside a buffalo. Bill fired a shot. The buffalo went down. Brigham carried him to the next buffalo and the next until Bill had killed all eleven with just twelve shots. The officers were stunned. Three wagons came and the hindquarters were loaded on. Then Bill presented the tongues to the five astonished officers.

So impressed were the army officers by the extraordinary buffalo hunter named Bill, that they couldn't stop talking about him. Thus Buffalo Bill and his Indian pony Brigham, riding for miles and bringing in thousands of pounds of meat, began to receive much publicity.

When the workmen on the Kansas Pacific Railroad saw him coming with load after load of meat, they'd say, "Here comes that Bill with more buffalo!" And they started a jingle:

"Buffalo Bill, Buffalo Bill
always aims and shoots to kill
He never missed and never will,
And the company pays his bill."

Bill wrote in his autobiography, "It was at this time the very appropriate name of 'Buffalo Bill' was conferred upon me by the road-hands. It has stuck to me ever since, and I have never been ashamed of it."

William Frederick Cody was born on a farm near LeClaire, Scott County, Iowa, on February 26, 1846. (In his early autobiographies Bill says he was born in 1845. He changed the date in order to add a year to his age because he wanted to join the army, but Bill corrected the date later.) Bill was the middle child of seven children born to Isaac and Mary Ann Cody. His sisters and brothers were named Julia, Eliza, Helen, May, Charlie, and Samuel. Bill was the only male child to survive to adulthood. He also had a half-sister, Martha, who was born to Isaac Cody and his first wife.

The railroad workers were certain to eat well when
Buffalo Bill was hunting for their dinner.

*The young William F. Cody was forced to work
a man's job long before his time.*

Bill liked to boast that he never went to school a day in his life, but he did. He went to school on and off throughout his youth and he learned his ABCs, but it was hard for him to sit still. He was more interested in outdoor activities.

Around 1849 gold fever hit Isaac Cody, and he wanted to rush to the California gold fields. Fear of Indian raids frightened Cody's partners and the trip was canceled.

When Bill was seven, his brother Samuel died from a horse-riding accident. It was a sad time for the family, and Bill's father, still yearning to go West, decided that now was the time to do so.

Many people thought that the United States Congress would open the territory of Kansas for settlement. Isaac Cody hoped this would happen and prepared his family for the move.

Bill went with his father to Salt Creek Valley, near Fort Leavenworth, Kansas, to stake a claim on the land, while his mother and sisters waited in Missouri.

At the fort, Isaac Cody traded with the Indians. One of the first trades he made was flour and tobacco for a little pony. Bill was thrilled and named the pony Prince. After a few hard falls and a lot of determination, Bill was able to break Prince for riding.

On May 30, 1854, the Kansas-Nebraska Act was passed by the Congress and approved by President Franklin Pierce. Isaac Cody got his land. Isaac and Bill built a log cabin, and the family was together again under one roof.

Salt Creek was the most beautiful valley Bill had ever seen. With his sisters, Bill picked raspberries, wild plums, crabapples, grapes, and corn. There were deer and wildlife all around them, and nearby a spring for water.

Bill was happy in his new home and liked watching the travelers on the Oregon Trail. Often trappers came along the trail with their pack animals and stopped to eat. One time, young Bill watched with fascination while they made bread. He'd never seen dough wrapped around a stick and held over the coals before. After it was cooked, some men invited him to join them. He was delighted to taste the bread and was surprised to learn that one of the men was a cousin, Horace Billings, who had been away for many years.

Billings made an impression on the boy with stories about his adventures on the wild plains. He had been a horse rider with a circus. He could ride standing up and was also an expert at roping cattle. Bill would remember these feats all his life.

*The Kansas-Nebraska Act enabled families
to move west and start farms they otherwise
may not have been able to afford.*

On the Fourth of July, 1854, Bill's father and some neighbors held a picnic and barbecue. They roasted beef in a pit. Local indians were invited too. They came dressed in fine feathers and buckskins. They did war dances, played Indian games, and ran horse races. Some of the neighbors gave speeches against slavery while others were in favor of it.

People called Bill's parents abolitionists because they were against slavery. Isaac Cody was not afraid to voice his opinion, but unfortunately his frankness made him a target for vigilantes.

When Bill was a young boy, he went with his father to Fort Leavenworth where his father gave a speech against slavery. Afterward, a group of drunken men stopped them and pulled Cody from his horse. They called him an abolitionist. Bill's father defended himself. He said he was not ashamed of his views, and he believed that Kansas should be a slave-free state.

Suddenly a man with a knife jumped out of the crowd and stabbed Isaac Cody in the side. Bill was horrified and swore to get revenge, but at that moment he had to care for his father. With help, Bill got him onto a wagon and held his father's head on his lap until they were home.

Mary Ann Cody nursed her husband back to health, but he was not out of danger. The anti-abolitionists were still after Isaac Cody. Disguised in a sunbonnet and shawl, Cody hid in the sod corn near the cabin. When he was strong enough to walk, he was moved 25 miles (40 km) away to Grasshopper Falls, but the men found out where he was hiding and were determined to shoot him. Bill hopped on Prince and tore off to warn his father of the danger. When Bill was spotted by the men, they chased after him. But his Indian pony was too fast for them, and he arrived in time to save his father. Still, the men persisted and one showed up at Bill's house. Bill held him back at gunpoint. The man left, but took Prince with him. Bill was very unhappy to lose his pony.

Isaac Cody died three years later. Bill suddenly found himself the man of the house.

2

SUPPORTING
THE FAMILY

Isaac Cody's death in 1857 left the family poor. Mary Ann Cody sold everything she could to pay off debts. In order to help, Bill went to work for a neighbor, driving an ox team to Leavenworth for fifty cents a day. This led to a job as an express boy carrying messages between firms for Russell, Majors, and Waddell's freight company.

When interviewing Bill, Mr. Majors asked Bill what he could do.

"I can ride as well as a man," Bill answered.

Mr. Majors hired Bill knowing that he needed the money to help out his family. The salary was from twenty to forty dollars a month, plus food, a place to sleep, and a mule to ride. But before Bill could work, he had to sign an oath.

"We, the undersigned wagon masters, assistants, teamsters, and all other employees of the firm of Russell, Majors, and Waddell, do hereby sign that we will not swear, drink whiskey, play cards, or be cruel to dumb beasts in any way, shape, or form."

Supposedly, Bill wrote in an X for his name. His mother was ashamed that her son couldn't write his name, so Bill promised her he would learn. He wrote William F. Cody wherever he found space, even on the sides of buildings, until he'd mastered it.

Whether or not Bill could write didn't matter to his boss. What mattered was how speedily Bill could deliver a message. Once he returned from an errand so quickly, one of the men thought that he hadn't even left.

His next job was as an "extra hand" on a caravan carrying supplies between forts. Freight wagons were as big as a room and could carry 7,000 pounds (3,150 kg) of food, furniture, clothing, and other supplies. There was one driver per wagon, and a train consisted of twenty-five wagons. The wagon master was in charge. Extra hands were needed, and Bill Cody was hired as one.

On one of the trips, Bill met "Wild Bill" Hickok, a handsome man ten years older than the young Bill Cody. Wild Bill was a scout and guide and he taught the boy many useful tricks about trailblazing. He advised young Bill to never pick a fight, but to always be ready to defend himself. It was good advice that Bill would remember.

The caravans traveled hundreds of miles from towns to forts. When Bill returned home after his first long trip, only his dog recognized him. Bill's hair had grown long, and he was dirty from head to toe. Hungry after being on the trail so long, Bill wanted to eat, but he wasn't allowed inside the house until he had bathed.

Legend says that Bill Cody shot an Indian at the age of twelve. Although it was to save another man's life, Bill was not proud or happy about the deed since he had many Indian friends. Still word got around of the young boy who killed an Indian.

Again Bill tried school, but much to his mother's dismay, he left after two and a half months to join a gold rush party heading for Pike's Peak country. No one in the group knew much about mining and, after two months, they gave up the search and returned home.

In April 1860, the Pony Express was born. At this time there was no way of sending mail except

Wild Bill Hickok and Buffalo Bill Cody both became legends of the American West.

To feed his family, Bill Cody would take many jobs. He was always happiest—and most successful—working outdoors.

by the Pike's Peak Express Company, which took twenty-five days from Missouri to San Francisco, or by stagecoach, which was quicker but unreliable. A map of the entire area showed a central route to be shorter and more practical. What was needed were fast horses and riders to make the trips.

Senator William Gwin of California suggested the idea of the Pony Express to Mr. Russell, who discussed it with his partners. The company of Russell, Majors, and Waddell had grown and acquired the Hockaday and Liggett Stagecoach line. The stage stops and the depots they used for their freight service provided them with natural delivery points for mail service. By adding more stations they could carry mail all the way to California—a distance of 2,000 miles (3,200 km). This route could be covered in ten days by fast horse riding, and the company advertised for riders.

Wanted
YOUNG SKINNY WIRY FELLOWS
not over eighteen. Must be expert
riders willing to risk death daily.
Orphans preferred.

At fourteen, Bill Cody became one of the youngest of the Pony Express riders. His first assignment was an easy one. He rode 45 miles (72 km), stopping at stations 15 miles (24 km) apart, and carried mail in a waterproof pouch slung under his arm. After two months, he received word that his mother was ill and went home to help her.

When she'd recovered he was back in action again, dodging Indian arrows and holdup men. "Wild Bill" Hickok had taught him to always be on guard, and he was. Legend says that when highwaymen wanted him to hand over a pouch he was carrying, he said, "Looks like you got the best of me." But instead of handing them the pouch, he twirled it around, knocked the men down, and galloped off too fast to be caught.

The Pony Express was popular for less than two years and faded away with the invention of the telegraph. (It was forgotten for years until Buffalo Bill brought it back in his traveling Wild West show.)

3

SOLDIER, SCOUT, AND JUSTICE OF THE PEACE

BILL WAS FIFTEEN when the Civil War broke out. The conflict over slavery had been going on since he was a child, but in April 1861, war was declared between the North and the South. Bill wanted to enlist in the Union army, but he was too young and his mother begged him not to. Instead he joined Chandler's Jayhawkers, a group of civilians who made secret visits at night across the border to Missouri. The Jayhawkers took horses from farms on the Missouri side and brought them to the Kansas side. Their aim was to get back the horses that Missourians had stolen from them earlier. Remembering that it was a Missourian who had stabbed his father, Bill thought that it was right to go along with the Jayhawkers. He still wanted to avenge his father's death. But his mother thought differently and put a stop to Bill's part in this activity, saying it was neither honorable nor right.

That fall, Bill carried military dispatches for the Union army between Fort Leavenworth and Fort Larned. In the winter he assisted in buying horses for the volunteer cavalry, and the next spring he served as a guide and scout during an expedition to the Kiowa and Comanche country on the Santa Fe Trail. They had some skirmishes with the Indians but no major battles. When he got home he found that Kansas was being terrorized by a group from Missouri much like the Jayhawkers. A home guard was organized called the Red Legged Scouts to protect Kansas residents. Bill joined the "Red Legs" for a short time until news came that his mother was ill again. He hurried to her side, and on November 22, 1863, Mary Ann Cody died. Bill took her death very hard and went to Leavenworth, Kansas, where there was a lot of excitement, to try and forget his grief.

While there he met several friends who were members of the Seventh Kansas Volunteer Cav-

This color poster shows all the jobs Buffalo Bill held during his fantastic career as a scout and guide.

alry Regiment. They urged Bill to join the army. So on February 19, 1864, William F. Cody joined the Union army. At this time, he was eighteen years old, five feet 10 inches (1.75 m) tall with brown hair and brown eyes. He soon tired of the boring army life and was pleased when he was put on detached services as a scout, changing from a blue army uniform to gray clothing.

In 1865 the Civil War ended. After his discharge from the army, Bill traveled to St. Louis to visit Louisa Frederici, "whom I adored above any young lady I had ever seen," he said. She was the cousin of a friend he'd met in the army. He was successful in capturing her heart. Bill was nineteen years old when they married in 1866.

Outdoorsman and conqueror of the plains, Bill Cody tried to settle down and be a good husband. For a while he ran the Golden Rule House, a hotel which had belonged to his mother, in Leavenworth. But being a landlord was too tame for Bill, and after six months he sold the business and headed for the frontier again.

The U.S. government was hoping to complete negotiations with the Indians for a permanent peace. A treaty was in the works, but it was taking time. Indian raids on the Kansas Pacific Railroad and settlements were occurring more often. Maps

Louisa Frederici became Mrs. Bill Cody.

of the frontier were rare, and guides who knew the territory were in demand. Bill was one of the best and was often employed as a scout and guide.

Back on the trail, he went to work for General William T. Sherman, the famous Civil War commander. The chief guide was Dick Curtis, a man who could speak the Indian language, but had a poor sense of direction. After traveling for hours through herds of buffalo looking for Council Springs and not finding it, General Sherman stopped and asked if anyone knew where it was.

Bill answered, "Yes, sir, I do. They're due south."

They were going due west at the time. General Sherman told Bill to lead on. For 12 miles (19.2 km) he rode next to the general, who said he had known Bill's father. From that time on they became good friends, and General Sherman would call on him many more times.

Another exciting and dangerous offer came Bill's way when a former boss of the Pony Express hired him to drive the stagecoach for the Overland Stage Line between Fort Kearney and Plum Creek. The pay was good, but it was a dangerous job. Small bands of Indian warriors, as well as bandits, were attacking wagon trains and stagecoaches.

At the time, drivers wore broad-brimmed sombreros, corduroy pants trimmed with velvet, and high-heeled boots. Each man carried a 9-foot (2.7 m) rawhide whip with a silver handle. Pulled by four horses, the teams went 8 miles (12.8 km) an hour. This job was perfect for Bill, and he wrote his wife that he'd be sending home his pay. She was happy to have the money but missed her husband and wished that he would adjust to city life. There wasn't much chance of that with the fast-growing frontier.

On December 16, 1866, a daughter was born to Bill and Louisa Cody. They named her Arta. Bill went to St. Louis briefly to visit his wife and daughter before going on to another adventure.

He went into partnership with William Rose to establish a town in Kansas. They called it Rome and hoped it would become the depot city. They built stores, saloons, hotels, and tent-houses, and they sold lots. When the town was completed, Bill brought in his wife and daughter, promising he'd soon be a rich man. Fearing Indian attacks, Bill slept sitting up at night, fully clothed and armed, but the Indians didn't come.

The town prospered awhile until a man named Dr. William E. Webb wanted to buy into the partnership. Cody and Rose turned him away. So Dr.

Webb moved only a mile (1.6 km) away and built Hays City. He promised employment with the railroad to anyone living there. It took only three days for everyone to move to Hays City and leave Rome deserted. Bill's first business enterprise was a failure, and he lost all his money. But Dr. Webb gave Bill two lots in the new town, and they soon became friends. Bill even took him buffalo hunting. It was soon after this that Bill earned the name Buffalo Bill.

In May of 1868, the Kansas Pacific Railroad line was completed. This brought more settlers to the frontier and complaints from the Indians that the settlers were taking their food. No farm or small village was safe from Indian attack. Because of his tracking ability, marksmanship, and bravery, Bill was called upon to find the Indians and stop them from further attacks.

It was not easy for Bill to fight the Indians. He was in sympathy with them for wanting to keep their land and sorry that the government treaties were broken. Yet, he also knew that there was no stopping the development of the West.

Some Kiowas and Comanches were on the warpath. Cody traveled 65 miles (104 km) from Fort Larned to Fort Hays to inform General Sheridan.

The Indians were respectful of nature and the
buffalo. They only killed what they needed
for survival. Buffalo Bill understood that
the Indian people were upset at the new settlers
and their treatment of nature, but Bill obeyed
his orders to fight the Indians.

When he got to Fort Hays, General Sheridan said that they needed a messenger to go 95 miles (152 km) south to Fort Dodge. Bill rested four hours, got a fresh horse, and took off, stopping only once for a fresh mount. After a six-hour rest at Fort Dodge, he rode back to Fort Larned with more messages. By the time he reached Fort Hays, he had gone a distance of 320 miles (512 km) in less than sixty hours. Because of his endurance and courage, twenty-three-year-old Buffalo Bill was made chief of scouts for the Fifth Cavalry. With the job came a house at Fort McPherson near North Platte, Nebraska. He sent for his family.

On November 26, 1870, Bill's only son, Kit Carson Cody, was born. Friends of Bill's suggested that he be named after the famous scout and trailblazer Colonel Kit Carson of the First New Mexico Volunteer Infantry. Bill nicknamed his son "Kitty."

Shortly after the birth of his son, Bill was made the justice of the peace for the town next to Fort McPherson, Nebraska. Knowing little of the written law, Bill made up what he wanted to say. While marrying a couple he said, "I now pronounce you man and wife, and whomsoever God and Buffalo Bill have joined together let no man put asunder."

Buffalo Bill really looked the part of a true westerner, an image he would stick with throughout his life.

With the Indians subdued, scouting came to a standstill. Bill needed to find other work. He and his friend Texas Jack began guiding hunting parties for famous people. Bill called them the "Millionaires Hunting Parties."

Dressed in his fur-trimmed buckskin coat and wearing a black slouch hat, under which his dark hair rested in ringlets on his shoulders, Bill looked like a true westerner. His outfit alone gave visiting Europeans a thrill.

On one occasion the Grand Duke Alexis, the third son of Alexander I, czar of all the Russias, decided to visit the West. General Sheridan organized a royal hunting party and got Bill to be the guide.

The hunt was very successful, and the duke awarded Bill with a gold stickpin set with diamonds, a Russian fur coat, and jeweled cuff links. Soon after the duke left, Bill was invited to New York for a visit. He wore the stickpin on the new tie he bought for the occasion. He didn't know he was headed for a new career.

THE ACTOR RECEIVES THE MEDAL OF HONOR

Everywhere Buffalo Bill went in the East, he was cheered. People thronged to see the Indian fighter of the plains. He was invited to parties and receptions and wore a dress suit for the first time. He was enormously popular and was always ready to tell a joke.

While in New York, he attended a play written by Ned Buntline called *Buffalo Bill: The King of Border Men*. When the audience knew the real Buffalo Bill was present, they demanded that he make an appearance, but Bill had stage fright and after only a few words, he left. Buntline, seeing how popular Bill was, offered him $500 a week to play himself on the stage. Bill refused, stating that he never could talk to a crowd. He said, "You might as well try to make an actor out of a government mule."

Meanwhile at Fort Hays, the fighting between the Indians and the settlers had started again, and General Sheridan summoned Bill to return. He dashed back and reported for duty.

With Texas Jack, Bill led a cavalry charge against a band of Sioux who had raided and killed three men at a nearby town. Bill found the fugitives' camp and recovered the stolen livestock. During the campaign, he was wounded in the head but kept fighting until the Indians were defeated. For his gallantry as an army scout in the Indian wars, the United States Congress awarded Bill Cody the Congressional Medal of Honor on May 22, 1872.

(It was unfortunate that in 1916 Cody's name was stricken from the record on the grounds that at the time of his actions Bill was a civilian and not a member of the military. He would have been pleased to know that the Congressional Medal of Honor was restored to him in June 1989, seventy-two years after his death.)

Bill Cody's bravery during war with the Indians was appreciated by the United States government. Here, both sides of Cody's Congressional Medal of Honor are shown.

The Congress to William F. Cody Guide for GALLANTRY at Platte River Nebr. Apr 26 1872

Admiring friends put Bill's name on the Democratic ticket for the Nebraska legislature. It was a complete surprise to Bill when he was elected. He was then called the Honorable William F. Cody. (Later he was given the honorary name of Colonel.) But Bill wasn't really interested in politics, and when he didn't show up at the capitol to claim his seat, the job went to his opponent.

A new daughter, Orra Maude, was born on August 15, 1872. Around this time a letter arrived from Ned Buntline urging Bill again to become an actor. Buntline enticed Bill with more money and said that shyness could be overcome.

Louisa Cody, anxious for city life again, encouraged her husband to take the job. Texas Jack was eager to try the stage and told Bill he'd go along. So Bill gave in, resigned his post with the cavalry, sent his family to live in St. Louis, and went to Chicago where he performed in the play, *The Scouts of the Prairie.*

On opening night of the drama, all the actors forgot their lines. Even the handsome twenty-six-year-old Bill Cody, dressed in buckskin and beads, just stared, tongue-tied, at the audience. Buntline, who was also in the play, thought he'd help by asking, "Where have you been, Buffalo Bill?"

Bill was staring into the audience and saw Mr. Milligan, whom he had taken on a recent hunting trip, sitting in the auditorium. "I've been on a hunt with Mr. Milligan," Bill said, and continued to tell how frightened Mr. Milligan was when he saw Indians. The audience loved the story and wanted more. It seems that Buffalo Bill was a hit by just being himself. The play grossed over $16,000 in one week. Bill gained confidence in himself and continued the season, ending up with money in his pocket.

The second season was a success, too. Bill then put on his own show, in which he replaced actor-Indians with real Indians. He called it *The Buffalo Bill Combination.*

At long last Bill bought his own ranch, Scout's Rest, on 4,000 acres (1,600 ha) in North Platte, Nebraska. He stocked it with fine horses and purebred cattle from England. And he had time to enjoy his favorite foods: wild meat, fresh soft-boiled eggs with bacon, sourdough toast, hot cakes, and coffee for breakfast; and for supper, chicken and dumplings, fried chicken, or broiled kidney, with custard pie for dessert.

Bill enjoyed being a rancher, but the theater paid well. Soon Bill was back performing in plays. Then the news came that his son Kitty had scarlet

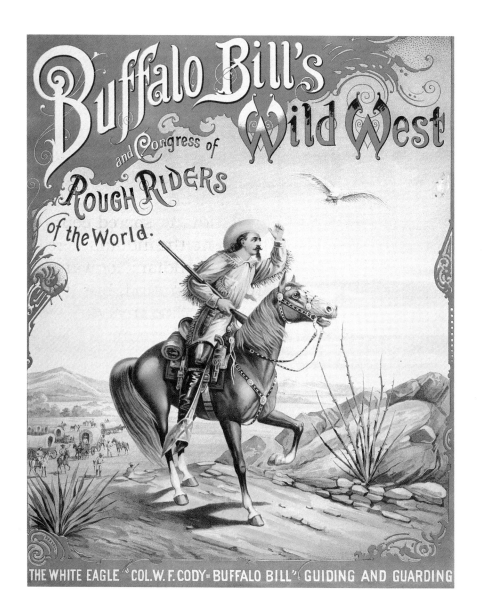

THE WHITE EAGLE "COL. W. F. CODY = BUFFALO BILL" GUIDING AND GUARDING

Buffalo Bill's stage career was well received by
millions of fans who became devoted to their hero.

fever. Bill left the show and returned home. He was heartbroken when Kitty died. After a while Bill decided to return to work in the theater. He had to do something to get his mind off the tragedy.

Then word reached Bill that the Indians were ghost dancing, which meant trouble was brewing. War with the Sioux was about to break out. Bill reported for duty at Fort Laramie. Gold seekers had invaded the Indians' sacred country along the Black Hills trail, and the Indians were in an uproar. No one blamed the Indians for wanting to defend their great hunting ground, but it was hoped they'd do it peacefully. The treaty of 1868 gave the Sioux, Arapaho, and Cheyenne the Black Hills country. The government promised that no white man would pass through without permission. General George A. Custer was sent to quiet the hostile Indians. Then the shocking news came of the defeat of General Custer and his men in the Battle of Little Bighorn.

The Indians were preparing for another battle. Eight hundred warriors left the Red Cloud reservation to join Sitting Bull in Bighorn Mountain country. Bill led a party of blue coats to War Bonnet Creek to head off two hundred of the warriors coming that way. With fifteen men, he galloped toward the oncoming Indians. One of the Indians

Although Bill Cody scalped Yellow Hand, other lives were probably saved, since the Indian warriors then retreated and a battle was avoided.

darted ahead. Bill recognized him as Chief Yellow Hand. Bill fired. At the same time his horse tripped and fell. Bill's shot missed and hit the Indian's horse. Yellow Hand fell to the ground and rolled so his horse would not fall on him. Both Bill and Yellow Hand jumped to their feet and fired. Yellow Hand's bullet missed, but Bill's found the mark. The Indian warrior fell into the dirt. In the heat of the moment, Cody yanked off Yellow Hand's war bonnet and quickly scalped the Indian. The two hundred Indians that were about to overpower him turned and galloped away.

After the Sioux War there were few Indian uprisings, and Sitting Bull soon withdrew to Canada, where he stayed out of reach of the U.S. Army for several years. Bill then went back to Rochester, New York, and another season of melodrama.

Prentiss Ingraham, who turned out hundreds of Buffalo Bill stories, also wrote advertising for the play. One announcement read:

BUFFALO BILL COMBINATION
(Hon. W. F. Cody)
Supported by Capt. Jack
The Poet Scout of the Black Hills
In the new drama founded on incidents
in the late Indian War

entitled
THE RED RIGHT HAND,
or
BUFFALO BILL'S FIRST SCALP FOR CUSTER.

It was a five-act play with a lot of action, but without much sense.

Following a tour of the eastern cities, Bill made the first of many announcements that he was going to quit show business. He told his wife that he would stay on the ranch, raise cattle, and write his memoirs.

5

A HERO TO MANY

HIS FIRST AUTOBIOGRAPHY was dictated to a secretary. Since he read little and had little schooling, Bill was not familiar with punctuation and spelling. Although he was a fast learner and studied hard, he still made mistakes. When his publisher complained about his punctuation Bill replied, "Life is too short to make big letters where small ones will do; and as for punctuation, if my readers don't know enough to take their breath without those little marks, they'll have to lose it, that's all."

Retirement did not last long. Soon he was back touring the West Coast with a small show of his own and thinking about how to enlarge it.

The stage was too confining for what he had in mind. A great outdoor show needed a large arena in which he could show the world what the Wild West was really like. There would be buffalo, horses, bears, Texas longhorn steers, bucking broncos, Pony Express riders, stagecoach drivers, Conestoga wagons, Indian tepees, chiefs and warriors, and real cowboys, not actors. It would be a show of childhood remembrances with horse racing and roundups and trick riding, as he remembered seeing his cousin Horace Billings do so many years ago. He filled six boxcars, two open cars, and two coaches with equipment. *Buffalo Bill's Wild West Rocky Mountain and Prairie Exhibition* held its first performance in Omaha, Nebraska, on May 17, 1883. It was an instant success.

Buffalo Bill, well over his stage fright, appeared in white-fringed and beaded buckskin and a white sombrero. He rode a white horse and carried a Winchester rifle. It was a thrilling pageant of the history of the West. Everything that he had experienced and observed since childhood was put in the show. Nothing was left out.

Buffalo Bill was a hero to many children. Once, a young boy named Johnny Baker, a lad of about twelve years old, asked to hold the reins of

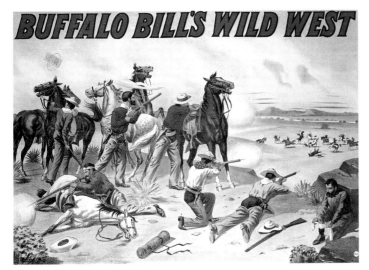

Buffalo Bill's Wild West show used real cowboys and Indians to show what the West was like. Here the Show entertains prisoners at Auburn State Prison in New York.

Buffalo Bill dressed to impress the many people who bought tickets for his latest extravaganza.

Bill's horse while Bill went into a store. When Bill came out, the boy was still there. Johnny Baker begged Bill to let him tag along. He explained that he could throw the glass balls into the air for Bill to shoot. Thinking that his Kitty would have been about the same age if he had lived, Bill adopted the fatherless child and took him on the road. He taught him shooting skills and gave the boy, called the "Cowboy Kid," an act of his own.

Another young person wanted to join, too. Annie Oakley was a small, slender woman of twenty-five and a crack shot with a rifle. She could shoot an apple from her French poodle's head, cigarettes from her husband's mouth, a dime held in his fingers, and she could slice a playing card in two. Bill thought she was wonderful and gave her the nickname "Little Missy." Although he had Johnny Baker's shooting act in his show, he added Annie Oakley's act as well.

Sitting Bull called Annie "Little Sure Shot." Bill was able to get the famous Sioux leader to join the show and to reenact the Battle of Little Bighorn by promising Sitting Bull that he could see Annie shoot every day. Everyone knew that Buffalo Bill and Sitting Bull had not been friends in the past. Even though a poster showed a picture of Buffalo Bill and Sitting Bull with the words "Foes in '76—Friends in '85," audiences still hissed at Sitting Bull wherever he went. The Indian chief soon tired of it and went home.

Buffalo Bill's Wild West show set sail for England in March 1887. Queen Victoria watched with delight and especially enjoyed Annie Oakley's perfect marksmanship. The next year the show went to Europe for another successful tour. Now Buffalo Bill was a millionaire.

For the first time in his life, Bill had plenty of money. He had six business projects of his own and dozens more that he financed for friends and relatives. He established the town of Cody in the northwest region of Wyoming and had schools, churches, and other buildings built. He also brought in a railroad to service it. The town's hotel, named after his youngest daughter, Irma, is still standing today. On the south fork of the Shoshone River, he built the TE ranch, named after the brand on his cattle. He successfully started cultivating sugar beets, and financed a large irrigation system between the Bighorn Mountains and Yellowstone Park.

Buffalo Bill was more famous now than he'd ever been. Everyone knew the handsome man with his silvery hair, goatee, and moustache. The Wild West show had traveled thousands of miles, and he was getting tired. "I'll make my farewell tour in 1900 and close at the World's Exposition in Paris," he told news reporters. But he didn't.

Poor business ventures drained his bank account. People took advantage of him because he was trusting. The onetime millionaire was soon penniless and owed money. He had to keep working. Friends tried to help. Children sent pennies, nickels, and dimes to their hero. Bill was so touched by this that he said, "I guess my life has been worthwhile after all."

Then he was tricked into selling his show. Buffalo Bill was still the star, but no longer the owner.

Still in need of money, he constantly thought of ways to earn it. With the growing interest in motion pictures, Bill thought about putting his show on film. With backing from the new owners of the Wild West show, Bill decided to film the Battle of Wounded Knee, in which Sitting Bull was accidentally killed and Indians and soldiers were massacred. He decided to use actual Indians and soldiers rather than actors. It was nearly a disaster. Some of the young warriors were planning to use real bullets instead of blanks in their rifles. They wanted vengeance for the deaths of their forefathers. Bill found out about it and called the old chiefs together to put a stop to the trouble.

Buffalo Bill loved children, and they
certainly loved him! (Facing page) This 1900 photograph
should have marked Bill's last tour,
but events would turn out otherwise.

Buffalo Bill saw many things change during his lifetime—from the horse-and-carriage rides he was so familiar with . . . to his first automobile ride.

A month shy of his seventy-first birthday, Bill was still trying to raise money for his show when he collapsed. His wife and adopted son, Johnny Baker, hurried to his bedside, although Johnny arrived too late. On January 10, 1917, the Honorable Colonel William Frederick Cody, also known as Buffalo Bill, died. He was buried on top of Lookout Mountain near Denver, Colorado.

When William F. Cody was born, there were twenty-eight states in the Union, and the population was 20,500,000. When he died, there were forty-eight states in the Union, and the population grew to 99,850,000. During the seventy-one years of his life, slavery was abolished, the first transAtlantic cable was laid, the first transcontinental railroad was completed, and Thomas Edison invented the phonograph, the electric light bulb, and the motion picture camera. Henry Ford built the first gas engine, and Wilbur and Orville Wright flew the first airplane.

Buffalo Bill saw it all.

The Scout, *a statue in memory of Buffalo Bill, stands atop Lookout Mountain.*

FOR FURTHER READING

Buntline, Ned. *Buffalo Bill: His Adventures in the West*. Salem, N.H.: Ayer Co. Publications, 1974.

Cody, Colonel William F. *Buffalo Bill's Life Story, An Autobiography*. New York: Rinehart & Co., 1920.

DiCerto, Joseph J. *The Pony Express: Hoofbeats in the Wilderness*. New York: Franklin Watts, 1989.

McCall, Edith. *Hunters Blaze the Trails*. Chicago: Children's Press, 1980.

Russell, Don. *The Lives and Legends of Buffalo Bill*. Norman, Ok.: University of Oklahoma Press, 1960.

Sell, Henry Blackman, and Victor Weybright. *Buffalo Bill and the Wild West*. New York: Oxford University Press, 1955.

Zadra, Dan. *Frontiersmen in America: Buffalo Bill*. Mankato, Minn.: Creative Education, 1988.

INDEX